Maxine,
from my h ...

Dr

Vicky L. W...

MW00768256

A Woman's Heart and Soul and the Beauty of God

Thoughts, Prayers, and Inspirations from the Heart of One Woman to the Hearts of Many

by

Vicky L. Wells

authorHOUSE™

1663 LIBERTY DRIVE, SUITE 200
BLOOMINGTON, INDIANA 47403
(800) 839-8640
WWW.AUTHORHOUSE.COM

First published by AuthorHouse 11/03/05

ISBN: 1-4208-8414-X (sc)

Printed in the United States of America
Bloomington, Indiana

This book is printed on acid-free paper.

Introduction

Within these pages are personal thoughts, prayers, inspirations, and ideas from a woman just like you.

God made women so similar. We think similar thoughts, pray similar prayers, and gain inspiration from each other, yet we are all unique.

I gained my own inspiration through the thoughts, prayers, and words of other women. It is my desire that by sharing my words with others, someone else will be inspired as well.

Throughout the book are blank pages to fill in with your thoughts and prayers, to reveal your own heart and soul.

May God Bless You

Shared prayers to the Lord, reveal the most intimate parts of a woman's soul.

Remember, we as women always have each other and most of all we have the enduring love of a caring Heavenly Father. He is always there to hear our voices, the voices of the single women, the wives, the sisters, the mothers and the grandmothers everywhere.

Who the Lord is to Me

He is,
  My Lord,
    My God,
      My Life,
        My Soul,
          My Breath,
            My Being,
              My Everything!!

Within a woman's heart lies a place for so many things. A place first for God, which automatically provides space for everyone else.

Therein lies love. Love for God, husbands, children, parents, friends and strangers. It even holds a place for home, nature, animals and all the beauty of God's creation.

A woman's heart can also carry pain, sorrow, concern, joy, peace, calm, gratitude, forgiveness, strength, and courage.

Women are not perfect beings as is no one else, but oh, what an honor to be given by God the ability to hold so much within the confines of one heart.

Help me come to you Oh Lord, in my times of doubt and sin, and know that you will cleanse me and renew my spirit.

Create in me a pure heart O God and renew a steadfast spirit within me

Psalm 51:10

Help me Oh Lord to remember how blessed I am and to always share those blessings with others. I praise you and give thanks for all you do for me.

And do not forget to do good and to share with others, for with such sacrifices God is pleased.

Hebrews 13:16

*Thoughts and Prayers *

_____

_____

_____

_____

_____

_____

_____

_____

_____

_____

_____

_____

_____

_____

_____

Lord,

Help me to be obedient to your revealed will so that I can also receive the secret will that only you know, your plan for my life. The one so glorious, I can't even imagine. I know I must become more obedient in the ways I see, before you can give me that which I cannot see.

Teach me to do your will, for you are my God, may your good Spirit lead me on level ground.

Psalm 143:10

As we all know, in these times, life is full of adversities. Everywhere we turn people are hurting.

Sometimes we as Christians don't understand why we have to suffer.

All through the Bible, Christians suffered all sorts of trials. Physical, emotional and even spiritual.

This is where many of us find ourselves today, but through it all we must always remember, God loves us and has a plan for us whether we understand it or not.

We not only have to remind ourselves of this, we also have an obligation to help others who are suffering.

Trust in the Lord with all your heart and lean not on your own understanding, in all your ways acknowledge Him and He will make your paths straight.

Proverbs 3:5-6

Therefore, since we have been justified through faith, we have peace with God through our Lord Jesus Christ, through whom we have gained access by faith into this grace in which we now stand. And we rejoice in the hope of the glory of God. Not only so, but we also rejoice in our sufferings, because we know that suffering produces perseverance; perseverance, character, and character, hope. And hope does not disappoint us because God has poured out his love into our hearts by the Holy Spirit, whom He has given us

Romans 5:1-5

Heavenly Father,

You know my prayers and the desires of my heart. Please help me to be patient and without worry. Help me to know you are working it out toward the `absolute good' for me. I pray Lord to be joyful in my long suffering and not to dwell in the pain of it. I know you love me, that is the most wonderful gift I will ever receive.

And we know that in all things God works for the good of those who love Him, who have been called according to His purpose

Romans 8:28

Dear Jesus,

Please help me to be meek and humble. I want to do small things with great love, your love. I thank you for coming to this earth and showing us real love , "Agape Love." I pray that one day the love I share with others can even slightly compare to the love you share with me. Your love is the power that pushes me forward.

Blessed are the meek for they will inherit the earth.

Matthew 5:5

*Thoughts and Prayers *

_____

_____

_____

_____

_____

_____

_____

_____

_____

_____

_____

_____

_____

_____

_____

_____

_____

_____

The world today is a difficult place to raise our children. They have so many outside influences. As parents we have all these wonderful thoughts of what we want our children to be, but sometimes despite our efforts they stray.

I have determined through my own experiences that prayer is so important. We must teach them in the way they should go and pray for them everyday. God listens to the heartfelt prayers of mothers. I know because he has heard mine. I thank him daily for the beautiful hearts of my children.

Love them, teach them, and always pray for them. These are some of the greatest gifts a parent can give to a child.

Love the Lord your God with all your heart and with all your soul and with all your strength. These commandments that I give you today are to be upon your hearts. Impress them on your children. Talk about them when you sit at home and when you walk along the road, when you lie down and when you get up. Tie them as symbols on your hands and bind them on your forehead. Write them on the doorframes of your houses and on your gates.

Deut. 6:4

A Letter to My Child

I have loved you since before you were born.

I have tried to show you by my words and actions just how much I love you, although many times I have fallen short. I pray your forgiveness for all the times I may have let you down.

To the best of my ability with God's help and all the strength of my body, mind, and soul, I have tried to give you love, shelter, food, and spiritual guidance. In this hectic world that has not always been easy, but I hope I have given all I could and that somehow most of all I have shown you the love God intended me to.

God has blessed me so much with your beautiful heart, your goodness, your faith, and your love. There are not enough words to express or describe how I feel about you, My Precious Child.

I have prayed for you since conception and I will pray for you until Jesus takes me home. I see his answered prayers in you every day that passes, and I give thanks. In the midst of my day I will think of you and I am filled with such joy that it seems my heart will overflow.

Remember always the Heavenly Father who created you from His love and then presented you to me so I could share in loving you. I will forever be in awe of the gift I have been given by Him. YOU!

Even when my time on earth is over the love I have for you, my child, will endure forever.
Thank you for being My Beautiful Child, My Beautiful Gift.

Lord.

Please help me to overcome my many fears. They keep me from going forward so that your plan for my life can be fulfilled.

Thank you, Oh Lord for your faithfulness and love that is always present in my life. I want to turn all my fears and worries over to you.

I sought the Lord and he answered me: he delivered me from all my fears

Psalm 34:4

I pray for a oneness with Christ like I have never known before. I want to feel and see more of Christ miraculous love in my life and the lives of my children. I want to taste, smell, and breathe what heaven will be like. It will be my most joyous day when Christ calls me home in His time. I love You Lord.

You have made known to me the paths of life; you will fill me with joy in your presence

Acts 2:28

*Thoughts and Prayers *

_____

_____

_____

_____

_____

_____

_____

_____

_____

_____

_____

_____

_____

_____

_____

_____

_____

_____

Lord,

I know I am in your waiting room now. Help me to be patient and understand that your plan will unfold for me when you know the time is right. I asked Lord that you would help me to be more disciplined while I wait. Please forgive my shortcomings and my failures. Help me to continue learning all I can from the waiting room, until the time your plan for me is fulfilled.

Be still before the Lord and wait patiently for Him

Psalm 37:7

I pray for the ability to not criticize my children. I want to be able to lift them up and inspire them. They are precious and special. God has touched them with His grace and mercy, because just like me they are not perfect. Help me Lord to remember that.

But to each one of us grace has been given as Christ apportioned it.

Ephesians 4:7

Lord,

I pray that somehow I have built a foundation for my children. You never know what they are doing when they are not in your sight, but I pray that the things of You Lord that I have tried to teach them will come through in how they live their adult lives. In Your Name I Pray.

Train a child in the way he should go and when he is old he will not turn from it.
Proverbs 22:6

My Precious Heavenly Father,

I know you are with me daily. I could not endure this world without your Holy Presence in my life. I am so needy and you know that. Thy Love, Oh Lord. Thy Security, Oh Lord. Thy Will, Oh Lord. Thy Heart, Oh Lord is my desire. Live and Breathe in me. Change me, make me whole and Holy in thy presence.

I will instruct you and teach you in the way you should go; I will counsel you and watch over you.

Psalm 32:8

Thoughts and Prayers

_____

_____

_____

_____

_____

_____

_____

_____

_____

_____

_____

_____

_____

_____

_____

_____

_____

I pray I can be drawn to obey you Lord with such a force within me that I cannot ignore it. That I will myself desire it so that it will be done. I want to please you but I have such a hard time letting go. Please give me the strongest desire to do Your will.

But if anyone obeys his word, God's love is truly made complete in Him.

1 John 2:5

Thank you Lord for the hills and the valleys. I know first hand how the difficulties in our lives can bring the most wonderful blessings, if we trust in you. Your love for me endures all my hardships and I am so grateful.

From the fullness of his grace we have all received one blessing after another

John 1:16

I pray I will become more faithful. I want to know that even through my tears my focus will remain toward Christ. Thank you Jesus for always bringing me through the pain and the tears, right to your open arms. I can't imagine a life without you in it. I love you so much.

The Lord is my rock, my fortress, and my deliverer, my God is my rock in whom I take refuge, He is my shield and the horn of my salvation, my stronghold

Psalm 18:2

Guide me, Oh Lord through this life. This life that confuses me and makes me feel lost. Without you I could never get through even one day. You are my light. No matter how dark the path may seem, your light always shines through to let me find my way. I love you.

I am the light of the world. Whoever follows me, will never walk in darkness, but will have the light of life

John 8:12

A Letter to My Grandchild

I dreamed about you when I found out you were in your Mommie's tummy.

I did not even know whether you were a boy or a girl, all I knew was that I already loved you.

The month's went on and we found out you were a boy.

I watched you grow inside your mommy and just felt that God was creating the most wonderful little being.

Finally the day came--you made your grand entrance into my life and it will never be the same again.

I look at you and feel so much happiness and love.

You can smile or cry or laugh and it makes me feel so much joy.

I did not think God could bless me more than He had when He gave me my children, but when He gave me a grandchild my world was complete.

You are Mamaw's Sweet Jaxson. You fill my heart and my soul with this overwhelming sense of purpose.

How special I am now--I am my Jaxson's Mamaw.

Remember how much God loves you and how special you are to all those you touch with your sweet, loving smile.

Dear Heavenly Father,
I know you have a plan for me that I can't begin to imagine. I ask forgiveness for all the things I do that delay the plan. I ask forgiveness for my disobedience. I know your faithfulness and I look forward to seeing the plan you have for me. Thank you for loving me and being patient with me, though I do not deserve it.

For we are God's workmanship created in Christ Jesus to do good works which God prepared in advance for us to do.

Ephesians 2:10

*Thoughts and Prayers *

_____

_____

_____

_____

_____

_____

_____

_____

_____

_____

_____

_____

_____

_____

_____

_____

Dear Lord,

Help me not to worry so much. I pray for a stronger faith. I know in my heart that you do work all things for the good of those who love you. Your love is the greatest love I will ever know. No matter what comes in my life you will always be there, loving me.

Who of you by worrying can add a single hour to his life? Since you cannot do this very little thing, why do you worry about the rest?

Luke 12:25-26

A Mother's Hands

A mother's hands are strong but gentle. She tends her children's wounds with those hands. She prepares their meals, does their laundry, and scrubs away the dirt from a days play. With those same hands she wipes away the tears from a days pain.

The hands given to a mother are the most special of all the hands God created. He knew how many lives they would touch.

A mother's hands are forever working to bring comfort to her children.

Her children arise and call her blessed

Proverbs 31:28

A Letter To My Mother

Mom you are so special to me. You have helped me see my capabilities, even when I am blind to them.

You have turned the ugly in life into the beautiful with the love you have shown me.

You have made me feel like a special person, friend, and daughter.

You are my greatest supporter. I can always count on you to encourage and uplift me. God knew you were special and that you would be the mother that I needed to help me grow and become independent.

He has blessed my life with a wonderful, loving mother. He knows your heart and mine and the two will forever be intertwined.

You're my confidant and my best friend.
God has helped us to grow in faith and in His Glory together.

I feel such pride in calling you Mama. God gave me that, because He knew how special you are, even when you do not realize it.

I want to thank you for who you are and what you have given to me. I will carry it with me always.

"Her children arise and call her blessed."

I call you blessed, now and always.

*Thoughts and Prayers *

_____

_____

_____

_____

_____

_____

_____

_____

_____

_____

_____

_____

_____

_____

_____

_____

Lord,
I pray to be able to have a quietness in my mind
so that, without distractions, I can be close to you.
My mind can tend to be my worst enemy. Lord I
want to be yours and not mine and not earthly
things that surround me. Only through You can I
find the true and pure peace of mind that I need to
be closer to You and all You offer to me. Peace.

Instead, it should be that of your inner self, the
unfading beauty of a gentle and quiet spirit, which
is of great worth in God's sight.

1 Peter 3:4

Help me Lord to realize that you are here and this is the task at hand right now in my life. There is a reason for all things, even the difficult things. Although so much of the time this feels like I am in a valley. I know one day I will be on the mountain top, all because of your love and your knowledge of what is best for me right at this moment.

Find rest, O my soul, in my God alone, for my hope comes from him.

Psalm 62:5

Lord,

Forgive me when I am cynical. Forgive me when I am influenced by the cynicism and immorality of others. Keep me on the path you have for me-- which is filled with hope, joy, and love. Help me not to be swayed by the painful words of others. Help me to know who I am in You.

No temptation has seized you except what is common to man. And God is faithful, he will not let you be tempted beyond what you can bear. But when you are tempted, he will also provide a way out so that you can stand up under it.

1 Corinthians 10:13

Do you ever asked yourself the question, "Am I growing wiser with age, or am I growing stagnant and passive? I think I am the latter. Has my spiritual growth come to a stand still?"

These are questions we all need to ask ourselves. It seems our lives are so busy and hectic that we do not take time to grow in the Word, which is where wisdom comes.

We grow older but we do not grow wiser. We become too comfortable right where we are.

Growing old is guaranteed, growing spiritually is a choice. I need to make the choice! I want to choose wisdom.

I pray God's wisdom will fill all our hearts so we can discern right over wrong in this world of tolerance, through the maturity given us by the Holy Spirit.

Teach us to number our days aright, that we may gain a heart of wisdom

Psalm 90:12

*Thoughts and Prayers *

Lord, for a while I dreamed of meeting a man who would love me, think of me as special, be my Mr. Wonderful. I had no preference any man would do.

Then as my faith became stronger, I dreamed of meeting a man who would love me, think of me as special, and be a good provider for me and my children, be my Mr. Wonderful.

Then as I matured in my age and my faith, I dreamed of a man who would love me, think of me as special, be a good provider, and a caring Christian man, be my Mr. Wonderful.

It seems I have spent my whole life dreaming of this man, but this dream has gone unfulfilled. Over the years this has caused me great sadness.

Lord I know that I may never meet this man, but I am okay.

I have aged some more, matured some more and realized that you are the man who loves me, thinks of me as special, provides for me and my children, and are not just a Christian, but the Christ, my Mr. Wonderful.

Help us remember God, we are all Your children. You know all our insecurities and that we are without the ability to understand the events of our lives. Help us to have faith in you, because you know all, understand all, and love us all with a love that surpasses all the troubles of our lives.

How great is the love the Father has lavished on us, that we should be called the children of God. And that is what we are! The reason the world does not know us is that it did not know him.

1 John 3:1

*I pray I can serve you Lord, right where I am.
I tend to think oh, I can't do this for You because
I haven't come to terms with some sin in my life.
I know from Your Word you love me right where
I am. I want to accept that I can serve you well
from this very place.*

*I press on toward the goal to win the
prize for which God has called me
heavenward in Christ Jesus.*

Philippians 3:14

*Thoughts and Prayers *

_____

_____

_____

_____

_____

_____

_____

_____

_____

_____

_____

_____

_____

_____

_____

Remember the seed God planted, the growth of a child in the womb of Mary. The birth of a child in circumstances we could not imagine. The willingness of Mary to endure the hardship, to fulfill a plan that even she did not fully understand, but was willing none the less to obey and accept it, in order that Gods plan could be fulfilled by using her to bring a little boy into the world who would be the Savior of all.

Place your cares on this child as He commanded. Give thanks daily to the Father and the Son for the sacrificial love they so willingly gave and lovingly give to us daily.

I can't begin to express the joy I feel when my mind, heart, and soul, travel to the place where God breathed life into that child born in Bethlehem. And then, breathed eternal life into all of us through that same child as he gave his life on a cross.

Thank you Lord for hearing my voice.

It amazes me everyday how much you love me.

I lift up my prayers and petitions and I feel you listening.

Words could never describe what I feel inside knowing how I am loved by You. It is too powerful, too miraculous, and too amazing to explain with my limited vocabulary.

My heart is so full with You, Lord. I will praise You all of my days!!!

Great is the Lord and most worthy of praise, his greatness no one can fathom

Psalm 145:3

Thoughts and Prayers

_____

_____

_____

_____

_____

_____

_____

_____

_____

_____

_____

_____

_____

_____

_____

_____

The

Beauty

Of

God

The beauty of God is in everything around us. It is in our thoughts, our sights, our feelings, nature, other people, and circumstances. We see His beauty throughout our day, but we have to be a tuned to it. The world gets so loud it drowns out the beauty.

If we believe in Him, we not only witness His beauty in our lives, we carry it inside ourselves.

I have written several instances where I have seen the beauty of God. I have learned over the years to recognize His beauty and understand that it is everywhere if I slow down and quiet my mind, He makes it quite clear.

The God who made the world and everything in it is the Lord of Heaven and earth and does not live in temples built by hands. And he is not served by human hands, as if he needed anything, because he himself gives all men life and breath and everything else.

Acts 17:24-25

When your sitting in traffic on the highway and you look ahead of the traffic to see the blue sky, lined by the green trees and mountain tops, this is the beauty of God.

When something horrible happens in your life, and you feel you can't get through another day, but you do, this is the beauty of God.

When you watch your children playing and you feel so thankful that they are healthy, happy, and enjoying life, this is the beauty of God.

When your husband looks at you with a softness in his eyes and says, "I love you," this is the beauty of God.

When your son surprises you by saying, "I love you," without you saying it first, this is the is beauty of God.

When your daughter surprises you by saying, "I love you," without you saying it first, this the beauty of God.

When anyone says' "I Love you," without you saying it first, this is the beauty of God.

When you have spent years praying for your child's salvation and one day you get the most awesome pleasure of hearing them say the words with love in their hearts, "I accept Christ as my Savior," this is the beauty of God.

When your sitting in the drive thru line at McDonald's and you notice the flower bed located between windows one and two, and you smile at how amazingly gorgeous they are, this is the beauty of God.

When after many hours of labor the doctor places that tiny bundle in your arms, and all your pain and exhaustion suddenly disappear, this is the beauty of God.

When you are in the mall and a child yells, "mama," and every woman turns to look, this is the beauty of God.

When you see someone hurting and in pain, and you feel their hurt and pain within your own heart, this is the beauty of God.

When you see an accident on the road and you immediately begin to pray for those involved, and their families, this is the beauty of God.

When you see your child giving birth to her child, and immediately you feel a bond with her you never imagined possible, this is the beauty of God.

When your teenage son has gone out and you have said prayers of protection and safety for him, and soon he walks through the door, this is the beauty of God.

When your teenage daughter has gone out and you have said prayers of protection and safety for her, and soon she walks through the door, this is the beauty of God.

Thoughts and Prayers *

_____

_____

_____

_____

_____

_____

_____

_____

_____

_____

_____

_____

_____

_____

_____

_____

_____

_____

When you hold your grandchild in your arms for the first time and he looks at you as if he already knows who you are, this is the beauty of God.

When your grandchild sees you from a distance and their eyes lock with yours and they come running with their arms wide open to jump into yours, this is the beauty of God.

When someone has hurt you and your mother says, "one day everyone will know, like I do, just how special you are," this is the beauty of God.

When an unexpected check comes in the mail, just when you are wondering how you will buy groceries this week, this is the beauty of God.

When you stand in your driveway with your head tilted back, looking up at the moon and stars, slowly turning in a circle, in awe of the sight, this is the beauty of God.

When you see an elderly woman having difficulty coming down a flight of stairs, and without thought or hesitation, you rush to assist her, and afterwards you feel a sense of peace, this is the beauty of God.

When a friend's husband is diagnosed with cancer and you witness her strength as she cares for him, this is the beauty of God.

When you sit on the bank of a flowing river and close your eyes as you listen to the sounds of the slow moving water and you feel as if there is nothing else in the world, just you and the river, this is the beauty of God.

When you walk along the beach, looking out over the massive ocean, with all its strange and mysterious creatures, and you wonder to yourself how God made all this, this is the beauty of God.

When you look at your precious children and wonder why God chose to bless you so much, and then you pause for a moment of complete gratitude, this is the beauty of God.

When you put the needs of others before your own, this is the beauty of God.

Thoughts and Prayers

_____

_____

_____

_____

_____

_____

_____

_____

_____

_____

_____

_____

_____

_____

_____

_____

When, after a long day at work you are greeted by your dog, and he is so excited to see you, and you wonder how an animal can love a human with such unconditional love, this is the beauty of God.

When you see an older child on the playground help a younger child up the ladder to the slide, this is the beauty of God.

When you've had a problem through the week and on Sunday morning you hear the preacher speak on the exact problem you had, and feel he is speaking directly to you, this is the beautyof God.

When you see young siblings hug each other and say, "I love you," this is the beauty of God.

When a child ask you where babies come from and you believe you should pray before answering, this is the beauty of God.

When anyone ask a question, you're not sure how to answer and you go to the Lord in prayer first, this is the beauty of God.

When you have lost a loved one and in the midst of the grief and mourning you smile because of remembering the joy they brought to your life, this is the beauty of God.

When you call a friend because she has been on your mind, and she's so glad you called because you have been on hers, this is the beauty of God.

When you look at the children of others and feel love and a sense of duty to them just as you do your own, this is the beauty of God.

When PMS sets in you begin to feel the usual sense of hating your life and everything in it, and right in the midst of the craziness you pray, "Help me Lord to remember it's just a few more days, and I will be sane again," this is the beauty of God.

Thoughts and Prayers

When you watch a child sleep and they truly look like an angel, this is the beauty of God.

When you have had several days of feeling fat and unattractive and become depressed about it, and then one night in the middle of your nightly prayers, you hear God say, "My child I love you just the way you are." this is the beauty of God.

When you roll a chair over your toe, and Satan tries to make you say an ugly word, but you don't. Instead you say, "Thank you Lord for helping me overcome temptation," this is the beauty of God.

When you hear a song of praise on the radio and you feel like only you and God are there, this is the beauty of God.

When you are in the car and you hear a song on the radio that touches your soul, and you raise your hands to God in praise, without regard to who may be watching from the car next to you, this is the beauty of God.

****

I have only touched the surface of all the places in life where God's beauty shines through.

In everything that happens, in each moment of our lives, we must always recognize that within it, the beauty of God is revealed.

*Thoughts and Prayers *

_____

_____

_____

_____

_____

_____

_____

_____

_____

_____

_____

_____

_____

_____

_____

_____

About the Author

Vicky Wells works full time as an Appeals Representative for a company in Marietta, Georgia. She is the mother of two children, Corey16 and Brittany 22. She is the grandmother of Jaxson 2 and step grandmother of Knox 4. As most women, she juggles her time between family, home, and work. In the midst of all this she makes time for her writing. (This is her first published work).

She has made her home in Dallas, Georgia for the last 12 years.

She is a Christian woman and loves the Lord with all her heart and soul.

Printed in the United States
39564LVS00006B/193-216